Treasures of Christ Church Cathedral
Dublin

SCALA

Introduction

From Viking boxes to medieval manuscripts, mummified animals to elaborate stone carvings, Christ Church has been the repository for an astonishing array of objects over the centuries. These tell the story of the many different phases of the cathedral's 1,000-year history, from its origins as Dublin's first cathedral, built by the Hiberno-Norse king Sitric Silkenbeard in around 1028. The story encompasses the medieval monastic years; the relative calm of the Reformation and subsequent turbulence of the Commonwealth period; the use of the crypt as a busy marketplace in the sixteenth and seventeenth centuries; and the major restoration of the whole building in the 1870s.

These objects connect us to the cathedral's past in a direct and tangible way, and often raise fascinating questions. In some instances their survival is truly remarkable; a tiny 2,000-year-old coin, only a centimetre wide, has outlived large stone buildings. They remind us of the centuries of skilled craftsmanship that contributed to the creation of the cathedral and the many different people who have passed through this extraordinary place.

Global Links and Local Finds

The range of objects linked with Christ Church is evidence of wide-ranging contacts with the known world, including Spain, Greece and Lebanon. Also among the items below is a selection of the diverse material discovered in the cathedral grounds over the years, particularly during archaeological excavations relating to the restoration of the cathedral in the 1870s and further excavations of the thirteenth-century Augustinian chapter house in 1886.

Widow's mite

The oldest object ever discovered in the cathedral grounds is the 'widow's mite'. This coin is over 2,000 years old, minted in Greece around 100 years before Christ was born. Its proper name is a 'Lepton' and it is worth very little in monetary terms, equating to just six minutes of a worker's daily wage at the time. The term 'widow's mite' comes from St Mark's Gospel, where it is recorded how Jesus watched a poor widow at the temple donating two such small coins. While the rich gave much larger sums, her donation meant more as it was everything she had.

Sitric penny

This coin, found in the grounds, depicts the Hiberno-Norse king Sitric Silkenbeard who, in around 1028, ordered the construction of Dublin's first cathedral on the Christ Church site. Around 30 years earlier, in c.995, Sitric had founded Ireland's first mint in the city and this penny represents Ireland's first indigenous coinage. Pennies of this type were produced c.1035–55, depicting a stylised representation of Sitric on one side and a cross with two hands on the reverse.

Roman figure of Venus

This extraordinary artefact is a figure of Venus chastising Cupid, found in the temple of Venus at Baalbeck. Baalbeck, once known as Heliopolis, is an ancient city in northeast Lebanon. Between 1898 and 1903, a German archaeological expedition excavated two of the temples at Baalbeck and reconstructed the ruins. It is unclear how this figure came to the cathedral but it may have been donated by a nineteenth-century scholar.

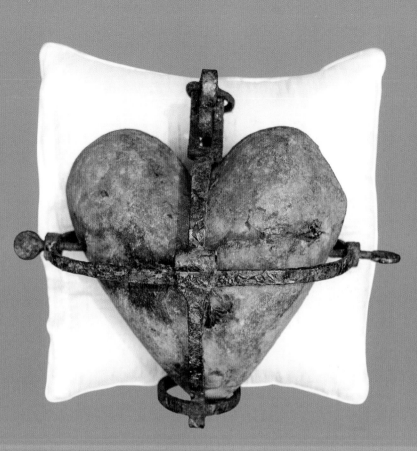

Heart associated with St Laurence O'Toole

This heart relic has long been associated with St Laurence O'Toole, the patron saint of Dublin, who also has strong links with Christ Church. He was consecrated archbishop of Dublin in 1162 at the cathedral's altar and resided in the cathedral monastery. St Laurence was canonised in 1225 and buried in Eu in Normandy, France, where he died. In 2012 the heart was stolen and remained undiscovered for six years, until its remarkable return to the cathedral in 2018.

Stone marbles

Marbles were originally made of stone and have been used in games for many millennia; Greek, Roman and Egyptian examples survive. This small collection of marbles, lost in the cathedral grounds over many centuries, includes a crude stone marble, a polished stone marble, clay marbles and a large glazed marble. They probably date from the fourteenth to the nineteenth centuries.

Viking box

The area around the cathedral has yielded an enormous quantity of ninth- and tenth-century Viking finds over the years. This simple wooden box is carved from a single piece of wood and has a distinct rebate for a lid.

Wig curler

This wig curler dates from the early eighteenth century and was used by a wig maker to curl hair – the curler would be heated in boiling water and a strand of hair then wrapped around it to the desired shape. This example was found in the cathedral grounds in 1886, during excavations in the area which once housed the old Four Courts. Christ Church hosted the judicial courts in its old monastic buildings from 1608 until 1796, when they moved to their current home in James Gandon's building, across the river Liffey.

A peruke maker's "wig-curler"
Site of the Old Four Courts
1884

J. New.

Bone sewing needle

Early needles made from shaped splinters of animal bone have been found in archaeological sites in Greece, Iraq, Turkey, Britain and Ireland. According to a note made when this needle was found in the grounds in the 1870s, it was possibly used for stitching shrouds. Its precise date is unknown.

Books and Manuscripts

Christ Church Cathedral has the longest continuous collection of records of any institution in Ireland, spanning almost 1,000 years. These reveal much about how the cathedral has changed over the centuries.

The Christ Church Magna Carta

Magna Carta or 'The Great Charter', one of the most famous documents in the history of the world, was created in June 1215. The Christ Church Magna Carta appears in a manuscript codex known as the *Liber Niger* or 'Black Book'. It was probably brought to Dublin by Henry la Warre de Bristoll, who became prior of Holy Trinity (commonly known as Christ Church) in 1301. The manuscript shows marks in the margin indicating clauses of Magna Carta that particularly interested the Christ Church canons.

Lantern slide of destroyed Christ Church deeds 1174

This lantern slide is all that remains of Henry II's confirmatic
grant made in 1174 by Richard de Clare, better known as St
of a parcel of land called Kennsalich (now Kinsealey, Co. Du
Hamund, son of Torkill. It is one of the few Christ Church dc
that specifically names Strongbow, despite his importance i
cathedral's history. He appears as 'Ric. Comes' (Earl Richard
again in the list of witnesses at the bottom as '[C]om. Ric de
(Richard Earl of Striguil). The original document was lost on
1922, when the Public Record Office of Ireland at the Four (
was destroyed in the opening engagement of the Civil War.

Liber Albus

The *Liber Albus* or 'White Book' contains copies of documents relating to Christ Church before the Reformation, compiled by the sub-prior, Thomas Fich, who reorganised the cathedral archives following a great storm in 1461. The book is open at a page recording a statute of 1493, which provided a stipend for a master to teach the four singing boys who had been appointed in 1480, the date associated with the foundation of the cathedral choir.

The Psalter of Christ Church, Dublin

The Christ Church psalter is an illuminated manuscript commissioned by Stephen of Derby when he was prior of Holy Trinity (commonly known as Christ Church) in the second half of the fourteenth century. The quality of its illustrations indicates the importance of Christ Church, the wealthiest and most prestigious monastic foundation in Ireland at the time.

These pages are examples of some of the finely painted miniatures used to decorate initial letters. One shows a group of monks singing from a lectern, to illustrate Psalm 149, 'O sing to the Lord a new song; sing his praise in the congregation of the faithful'. It emphasises the importance of music in the priory. The other illustrates Psalm 69, 'Save me O God, for the waters have come up'.

The accounts of proctor Peter Lewis 1564–65

The appointment of Peter Lewis as proctor (financial steward) in 1564–65 may have been due to his extensive building experience. This was a time when much of the cathedral was being reconstructed, after the nave roof and south wall collapsed in 1562.

This page in the cathedral accounts records an accident on 15 October 1565 at the Dodder quarry, where Lewis's workmen were gathering stone: 'This day there fell a great bank of earth in the quarry and over one mason ... [so] that we must draw him by the legs out of the earth. And he bled at the nose and the mouth ... but we saved his life with great to-do'.

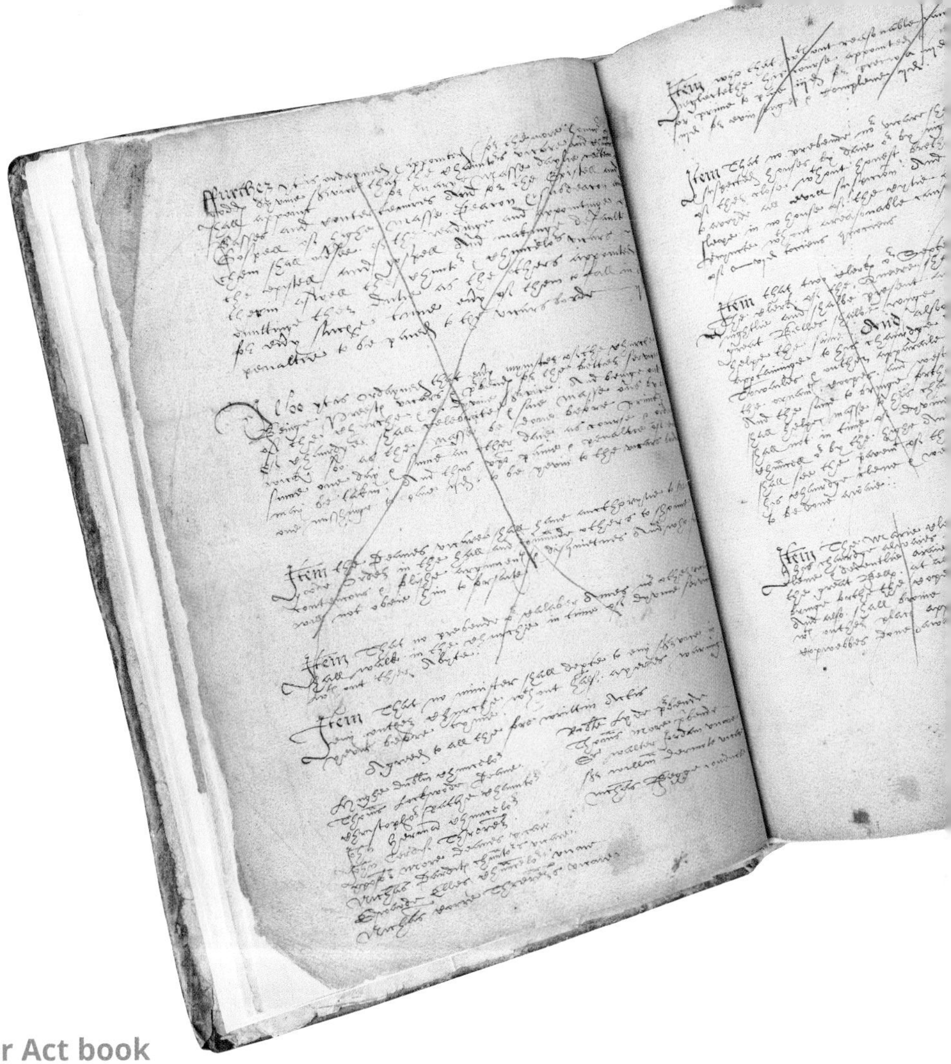

Chapter Act book

After the Reformation Christ Church was re-established as a secular cathedral, shedding its monastic obligations, and the Augustinian prior and canons became the dean and chapter. The new chapter recorded its administrative decisions in a series of Chapter Act books. The Chapter Act book pictured above is the oldest still surviving and covers the period 1574–1634.

Nuremberg chest

This heavy iron chest was originally used to store valuable items and documents. It dates from the mid-seventeenth century and was probably manufactured in southern Germany, around Nuremberg, where this style of chest was first made. Traditionally these chests belonged to government officials or churches. They are fitted with numerous locks, meaning that several keyholders had to be present to open them; the Christ Church Nuremberg chest has four locks. It is specifically mentioned in the cathedral records of July 1688 when it was used to transport important papers to safety in England.

Book clasp

This metal book clasp, found in the grounds, is evidently from a substantial book, which may have come from the cathedral's medieval library. It is decorated with a depiction of the coronation of the Blessed Virgin Mary. Originally the clasp would have had precious stones or enamelwork decorating the five ovals. It probably originated in Italy or Spain and may date from the fourteenth or early fifteenth century.

Ancient seal of the convent of the Holy Trinity Dublin, 1230, modelled from the ancient seal in the Record Office

The Christ Church Cathedral seal originated in the thirteenth century as a way of authenticating charters, leases and other documentation produced by the cathedral authorities. This is a replica of the earliest version of the seal, dating to 1230.

1660 cathedral seal

This seal represents a reworking of the design from 1660.

Church Plate and Liturgical Items

The cathedral has a substantial collection of beautiful and historic plate, some of it with royal links and all of it intended for use in the cathedral's major liturgical celebrations. Most of it is silver or silver-gilt; the brass candlesticks used during James II's visit form a significant and telling exception.

Silver bird for holding chrism oil

This unusual silver vessel, in the form of a pheasant with hinged wings and a removable head, was probably designed as a secular table ornament. It later came into the possession of the church's Ministry of Healing and was used to hold chrism oil for anointing. Its date of manufacture is unknown but it bears an import mark for 1904.

Williamite plate

This beautiful collection of silver-gilt altar plate was commissioned by William III (also known as William of Orange) for use in his royal chapel in Dublin. It was made by the London goldsmith Francis Garthorne in 1698–99. At this period Christ Church Cathedral functioned as both a cathedral and the Chapel Royal. However, it is unclear whether this plate was given to the cathedral or to the king's chapel in Dublin Castle.

James II tabernacle and brass candlesticks

Christ Church has been an Anglican cathedral since the dissolution of the cathedral-priory in 1541. For a brief time in 1689–90, however, the cathedral reverted to Roman Catholicism under James II. Father Alexius Stafford, one of James's private chaplains, celebrated mass for the king at the cathedral in 1689, when James came to Ireland to try to recover his kingdoms.

These are the plain brass candlesticks and the wooden tabernacle – for storing the consecrated bread and wine – used by Dean Stafford during this mass. Neither he nor James II knew that the silver plate (pictured opposite) usually used during services lay hidden beneath his feet.

1683 plate

This collection of plate was purchased by the cathedral in 1683. In 1689 it was buried for over a year under the coffin of Thomas Cartwright, Bishop of Chester, in order to protect it during a period of political unrest.

Cottingham's silver verge

In 1690, this silver verge – the staff of office of the cathedral verger, used when processing to the altar for services – was presented by Captain James Cottingham, a city goldsmith, captain of the Dublin city militia and a cathedral tenant. The verge is inscribed 'This Virge given to the Church by Capt Ja Cottingham in lieu of arrears of Rent of Colfabias. Act of Chapter accepting 8th January 1690'. The name 'Colfabias' refers to an area south of the old chapter house used as a toilet by the Augustinian canons. The verge is still in use today.

Communion host box

This round box was used to hold communion hosts for the daily Eucharist at the cathedral. It bears the inscription 'Part of Christ Church built by Sitricus, King of the Ostmen. Dublin 1038'. It probably dates from the 1870s restoration of the cathedral, using wood from the old cathedral roof structure.

Miniature chalice and paten

Erasmus Cope, the silversmith and churchwarden of St Werburgh's church (today part of the Christ Church Cathedral group of parishes) presented this miniature chalice and paten in 1717. The chalice is approximately 13 cm high, the paten approximately 8 cm in diameter. They were used for the administration of the sacrament in private houses at times of sickness. On 11 November 1837 the chalice and paten were stolen from the church by William Doolan or Dunn. He was transported from Ireland for seven years for this crime.

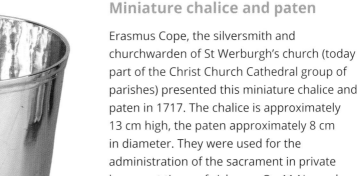

Burials

Over 1,500 people are known to have been buried throughout the cathedral building and grounds over the centuries. During the restoration of the cathedral in the 1870s, 10,000 cartloads of bones were removed from the crypt.

Strongbow monument

This black marble tomb marks the resting place of Richard de Clare, better known as Strongbow, who was buried at Christ Church in 1176. Strongbow was a nobleman and mercenary soldier who led one of the Anglo-Norman armies that landed off the coast of Ireland in 1169 and 1170.

Strongbow's ruthless landgrab and quick rise to power after his arrival in Ireland brought about a curious Dublin custom. According to this tradition any deal agreed under Strongbow's stern, watchful eye was legally binding. As a result, his tomb at Christ Church became an important place at which to do business. When it was accidentally damaged in 1562, after the nave roof fell in, a replacement was quickly found.

The monument standing in the cathedral today is this substitute, thought to have been taken from St Peter's churchyard in Drogheda, and depicts an anonymous fourteenth-century knight. The worn areas on his face and at the top of his head mark the spots where businessmen tested the coins they exchanged.

Kildare monument

This magnificent tomb, commemorating the nineteenth earl of Kildare, was commissioned by his wife Marie in 1746 from the London-based sculptor Henry Cheere. To a late eighteenth-century audience, accustomed to neoclassical costume, the use of ordinary clothing in place of togas and laurel wreaths would have been surprising. But the care with which Cheere has carved the ermine tips of the earl's cloak and the wrinkles in his son's stockings are a wonderful record of the dress of the period, as well as a touching tribute to his family life. Above it and attached to one side of the monument is the Kildare family crest, which unusually includes a monkey. This relates to a story about the family's pet monkey rescuing the first earl from a fire in the mid-thirteenth century.

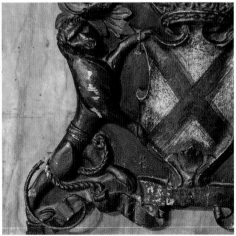

Tomb of Archbishop John Cumin

This tomb in the cathedral's south transept is thought to be the tomb of John Cumin (or Comyn), second archbishop of Dublin, who died in 1212. He was responsible for overseeing much of the cathedral's construction between c.1186 and 1210.

Monument to an unknown woman

This monument of an unknown woman, also in the south transept, dates from the late thirteenth or early fourteenth century. Tombs commemorating women are unusual at Christ Church and this is the finest surviving example.

Monument to the Agard and Harrington families

This alabaster monument is one of the most important Tudor sculptures to survive in Ireland. It memorialises Francis Agard and his daughter Cecilia Harrington and at some point was painted to resemble wood. Commissioned in 1584 by Cecilia's husband Henry Harrington, it is most likely the work of Gheerart Janssen the elder (d. 1611), who was one of a school of Dutch sculptors who settled in Southwark, London. The Agard family were members of the ruling elite in Ireland and Francis was regarded as Lord Deputy Henry Sidney's right-hand man.

The Old Building

The cathedral building replaced a Hiberno-Norse church on the site and is thought to have been built over the course of about 30 years from around 1186. Parts of this medieval building are still intact, especially in the two transepts, or 'arms', of the cathedral. A variety of other objects also survive from before the 1870s, when the building was extensively restored.

Fragments of medieval stonework

Many pieces of cut Dundry stone like these were stored in the crypt following the cathedral's restoration. They date from *c.*1180–*c.*1210. Where the pieces were located is hard to determine.

The examples here include the keystone of an arch with a human face in the centre, made to bite one of the mouldings, and a monster head capital, also known as a 'column swallower' (the mouth is carved so that it appears to be swallowing the shaft of the column below).

Nave head stop

The head stops and decorated capitals above the arches of the north wall of the nave date from around the 1240s–60s. One of the designs is a grinning monkey.

Stone capitals in the north transept

The medieval stonework found in the cathedral's north transept probably dates from the 1180s and is among the earliest surviving sculpture in Dublin. The lively scenes which decorate the tops of the stone capitals include attacking griffins (pictured), fruit pickers, sheep and shepherds, and a group of dancing musicians.

Seventeenth-century long choir woodwork

Very little remains of the old long choir, which was demolished during the 1870s restoration of the cathedral; the area had already been altered on numerous occasions since medieval times. This piece of finely carved and moulded woodwork may date from 1679–80 and has traces of gilding.

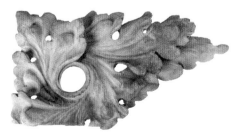

Medieval floor tiles

A number of tiles dating from the late thirteenth or early fourteenth century survive at the cathedral. It appears to have had its own kiln from at least 1343, though some suggest that this was in fact a bread oven. The distinctive 'foxy friar' Victorian tiles throughout the cathedral were reproduced in the 1870s from a single surviving medieval tile, now in the chapel of St Laud.

Baptismal font

This stone baptismal font, which dates from around 1500, is now housed in the cathedral crypt. It was used for the baptism of a grandson of Oliver Cromwell, whose campaign in 1649 and 1650 is one of the most controversial chapters in Irish history.

Wooden lions

The larger crowned lion comes from the cathedral's royal or state pew and dates from the reign of Charles II (1661–85), probably to when the pew was remodelled in c.1679. The second lion may date from an earlier royal coat of arms.

Medieval lectern

One of the finest items in the cathedral's collection is this medieval lectern, which dates from the period 1490–1520. Cathedral accounts from 1542 list a payment of 1s and 6d for a year's worth of 'cleaning the eagle and both pairs of great candlesticks'. During the turbulent decade of the 1650s, the lectern was removed from the cathedral and hidden for several years. By the early nineteenth century it had been painted brown and grained to simulate oak; it was restored to its original state in 1910.

Stocks

These stocks are over 300 years old. Made around 1680, they stood outside the cathedral in Christ Church yard until 1821. It was within the dean of the cathedral's powers to sentence any wrongdoers in the 'liberty', the area around Christ Church, to time in the stocks, where they could be pelted with rotten fruit and vegetables by passersby.

Charles I and II

These two statues of Kings Charles I and Charles II are thought to be the oldest surviving non-religious statues in Ireland; they were carved in 1683 by the Dutch artist Willem de Keyser. They once stood in niches above the door of the old City Hall, or Tholsel as it was known, which was situated opposite the cathedral. The Tholsel was demolished in *c.*1809. The two figures, and the royal coat of arms displayed with them, are the only features of the Tholsel to survive.

Two swords

These broken swords relate to one of the cathedral's more gruesome legends. One sword is said to have been used by a young soldier accidentally locked in the crypt after the funeral of his commanding officer, Sir Samuel Auchmuty, in 1822. Having lost his way in the warren of piled-up coffins after the funeral service had finished, the soldier was left behind and devoured by rats. He was apparently found some time afterwards, still grasping his sword.

The tale takes a final strange twist when, in the 1950s, one of the cathedral vergers caught a boy running out of the grounds with a broken sword. He brought it back to the cathedral to hang it up in the Chapter House, where it was displayed, only to discover that the original sword was still in place. The mysterious appearance of this second, identical, weapon has never been explained.

Cat and rat

Two of the most well-known objects in the Christ Church collection are the mummified cat and rat. They were discovered trapped inside the cathedral organ when it was dismantled and moved during the 1870s restoration. They are assumed to have got stuck after a chase around the cathedral, when the rodent dived into the organ to escape and the cat followed. They were naturally preserved and mummified inside the organ case.

Restoration

Between 1871 and 1878, Christ Church underwent dramatic and much-needed renovations, financed by the Dublin whiskey distiller Henry Roe and under the direction of the architect George Edmund Street. Inspired by his faith and backed by the huge profits from his whiskey distillery – the largest in the world at the time – Roe invested £220,000 (around €30 million in today's money) to completely restore the building. While significant features of the old building were maintained, many changes were also made. As a result, the cathedral today is a mix of medieval and Victorian architecture.

Details of head capitals of Street, Roe and a worker with palsy

These head capitals were carved during the 1870s restoration. They include portraits of the restoration architect George Henry Street and the whiskey distiller Henry Roe, who funded the project.

Further down the nave, other capital portraits were added. Their identities are now unknown but they may represent masons who worked on Street's restoration. This man appears to have suffered from a stroke or some kind of palsy.

Street & Seymour *Christ Church Cathedral: An Account of the Restoration*, 1882

This account of the restoration of Christ Church Cathedral, with a beautiful red and gilt decorated vellum cover, was written by the architect George Edmund Street and Edward Seymour to celebrate the project's completion. It is unclear how many of these books were printed. According to some sources, many unsold copies, together with the printing plates, were destroyed in a fire soon after the book was first produced.

SOUTH TRANSEPT (LOOKING EAST) FROM SOUTH AISLE OF NAVE.

here. The triforium and clerestory are very enriched compositions, the former having round and pointed arches combined, the latter none but round arches, and both are enriched with chevron mouldings.

CHRIST · CHURCH · CATHEDRAL

DUBLIN

Photographs of the restoration

These images are a selection from a group of photographs taken during the restoration by Millard and Robinson. One shows a group of men in top hats surveying work-in-progress on the new baptistery. The other shows the back of the cathedral from Winetavern Street, with a row of shops and houses which have since been demolished.

Henry Roe's walking stick

This badly damaged, silver-tipped walking stick was made in 1876 from a piece of oak taken from the cathedral's old wooden roof, which was replaced by stone vaulting. The inscription reads 'Oak out of Christ Church Cathedral at its rebuilding in 1876, Supposed to be 800 Years old'. The original owner was probably Henry Roe, who underwrote the cost of the restoration.

Vinaigrette

A vinaigrette is a small box with a hinged lid and grill, containing a sponge soaked in sweet-smelling oil. From the late eighteenth century, vinaigrettes were carried and used for inhaling to mask unpleasant odours. They were often exchanged between couples as a sign of affection. This vinaigrette belonged to Mrs Henry Roe – probably Roe's mother – and is engraved with her address.

The 1870s cathedral keys

A number of gothic-inspired keys survive in the cathedral collection and some are still in daily use, despite being over 140 years old. They were probably made by the expert metal-worker James Leaver of Maidenhead, England, to the precise designs of the restoration architect George Edmund Street. It was once said of Street that 'he would not even let his assistants design a keyhole'.

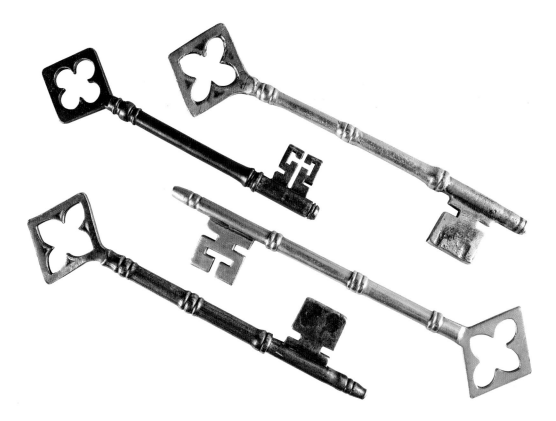